SCIENCE PROJECTS

Chemistry

Natalie Rompella

Heinemann
LIBRARY

www.heinemann.co.uk/library
Visit our website to find out more information about Heinemann Library books.

To order:
☎ Phone 44 (0)1865 888066
▤ Send a fax to 44 (0)1865 314091
▣ Visit the Heinemann Library Bookshop at www.heinemann.co.uk/library to browse our catalogue and order online.

First published in Great Britain by Heinemann Library, Halley Court, Jordan Hill, Oxford OX2 8EJ, part of Pearson Education. Heinemann Library is a registered trademark of Pearson Education Ltd.

Produced for Pearson Education by
White-Thomson Publishing Ltd.
Bridgewater Business Centre, 210 High Street, Lewes, East Sussex BN7 2NH

Editorial: Harriet Brown
Design: Tim Mayer and Alison Walper
Illustrations: Cavedweller Studio
Picture Research: Amy Sparks
Production: Duncan Gilbert

Originated by Modern Age
Printed and bound in China by Leo Paper Group

ISBN 978 0 431 04038 7 (hardback)
12 11 10 09 08
10 9 8 7 6 5 4 3 2 1

ISBN 978 0 431 04045 5 (paperback)
12 11 10 09 08
10 9 8 7 6 5 4 3 2 1

British Library Cataloguing in Publication Data
Rompella, Natalie
Chemistry. – (Science projects)
540
A full catalogue record for this book is available from the British Library.

Acknowledgements
The author and publishers are grateful to the following for permission to reproduce copyright material: Martyn Chillmaid, **pp. 12, 20**; Corbis, **title page** (Paul Steeger/zefa), **36** (Rolf Bruderer); Istockphoto.com, **pp. 6** (Amanda Rohde), **16** (Samantha Grandy), **18** (Graça Victoria), **24** (Eugeny Shevchenko), **28** (Victor Kapas), **31** (Vera Bogaerts), **32** (Ralf Stadtaus); **40** (Arunas Klupsas); Masterfile/Andrew Douglas **p. 4**; Science Photo Library, **p. 8** (CNRI)

Cover photograph reproduced with permission of Alex Kalmback/iStockphoto

The publishers would like to thank Sue Glass for her assistance in the preparation of this book.

Every effort has been made to contact copyright holders of any material reproduced in this book. Any omissions will be rectified in subsequent printings if notice is given to the publishers.

Disclaimer
All the Internet addresses (URLs) given in this book were valid at the time of going to press. However, due to the dynamic nature of the Internet, some addresses may have changed, or sites may have changed or ceased to exist since publication. While the author and publishers regret any inconvenience this may cause readers, no responsibility for any such changes can be accepted by either the author or publishers.

Contents

» Any words appearing in bold, **like this,** are explained in the glossary.

Starting your science investigation

A science investigation is an exciting challenge. It starts with an idea that you can test by doing experiments. These are often lots of fun to do. But it is no good just charging in without planning first. A good scientist knows that they must first research their idea thoroughly, work out how they can test it, and plan their experiments carefully. When they have done these things, they can happily carry out their experiments to see if their idea is right.

Your experiments might support your original idea or they might shoot it down in flames. This doesn't matter. The important thing is that you will have found out a bit more about the world around you, and had fun along the way. You will be a happy scientist!

In this book, you'll look at nine science investigations involving chemistry. You'll be able to discover some wonderful things about the world you live in.

Do your research

Is there something about chemistry you've always wondered about? Something you don't quite understand but would like to? Then do a little research about the subject. Go to the library and find some books about the subject. Books written for students are often a very good place to start.

Use your favourite Internet search engine to find reliable online resources. Websites written by museums, universities, newspapers, and scientific journals are among the best sources for **accurate** research. Each investigation in this book has some suggestions for further research.

You need to make sure that your resources are reliable when doing research. Ask yourself the following questions, especially about the resources you find online.

The investigations Background information

The start of each investigation contains a box like this.

Possible question

This question is a suggested starting point for your investigation. You will need to adapt the question to suit the things that interest you.

Materials needed

Make sure you can easily get all of the materials listed and gather them together before starting work.

Possible hypothesis

This is only a suggestion. Don't worry if your hypothesis doesn't match the one listed here. Use your imagination!

Level of difficulty

There are three levels of investigations in this book: Easy, Intermediate, and Advanced. The level of difficulty is based on how long the investigation takes and how complicated it is.

Approximate cost of materials

Discuss this with your parents before starting work. Don't spend too much.

1) How old is the resource? Is the information up to date or is it very old?

2) Who wrote the resource? Is the author identified so you know who they are, and what qualifies them to write about the topic?

3) What is the purpose of the resource? A website from a business or pressure group might not give balanced information, but one from a university probably will.

4) Is the information well documented? Can you tell where the author got their information from so you can check how accurate it is?

Some websites allow you to "chat" online with experts. Make sure you discuss this with a parent or teacher first. Never give out personal information online. The "Think U Know" website at http://www.thinkuknow.co.uk has loads of tips about safety online.

Once you know a little more about the subject you want to investigate, you'll be ready to work out your scientific question. You will be able to use this to make a sensible **hypothesis**. A hypothesis is an idea about why something happens that can be tested by doing experiments. Finally, you'll be ready to begin your science investigation!

It is important to protect your eyes, skin, and clothes when you handle chemicals.

What is an experiment?

Often when someone says that they are going to do an experiment, they mean they are just going to fiddle with something to see what happens. But scientists mean something else. They mean that they are going to control the **variables** involved in a careful way. A variable is something that changes or can be changed. Independent variables are things that you deliberately keep the same or change in your experiment. You should always aim to keep all the independent variables constant, except for the one you are investigating. The dependent variable is the change that happens because of the one independent variable that you do change. You make a fair test if you set up your experiment so that you only change one independent variable at a time. Your results are valid if you have carried out a fair test, and recorded your results or observations honestly.

Often, you want to compare one group with another to see what happens. For example, if you wanted to test what makes iron rust, you might use 10 iron nails. You would put five of them in a dry place (Group A) and five of them in water (Group B). Group A is your **control** group and group B is your test group. You would be looking to see if there is a difference between the two groups. In this experiment, the water is the independent variable. The effect of the water on the iron nails is the dependent variable.

You must do experiments carefully so that your results are accurate and reliable. Ideally, you would get the same results if you did your investigation all over again.

Your hypothesis

Once you've decided on the question you're going to try to answer, you then make a scientific **prediction** of what you'll find out in your science project.

For example, if you wonder why so many ingredients are added to chocolate chip biscuit dough, your question might be, "Is bicarbonate of soda really needed in chocolate chip biscuits?" Remember, a hypothesis is an idea about why something happens, which can be tested by doing experiments. So your hypothesis in response to the above question might be, "Bicarbonate of soda is needed in chocolate chip biscuits to make them rise." With a hypothesis, you can also work out if you can actually do the experiments needed to answer your question. Think of a question like: "How much acid is in your stomach?" It would be impossible to support your hypothesis, however you express it. This is because you can't possibly measure the amount of acid in your stomach. So, be sure you can actually get the **evidence** needed to support or disprove your hypothesis.

Keeping records

Good scientists keep careful notes in their lab book about everything they do. This is really important. Other scientists may want to try out the experiments to see if they get the same results. So the records in your lab book need to be clear and easy to follow. What sort of things should you write down?

It is a good idea to write some notes about the research you found in books and on websites. You should also include the names of the books or the web addresses. This will save you from having to find these useful resources all over again later. You should also write down your hypothesis and your reasons for it. All your **data** and results should go into your lab book, too.

Your results are the evidence that you use to make your conclusion. Never rub out an odd-looking result or tweak it to "look right". An odd result may turn out to be important later. You should write down *every* result you get. Tables are a really good way to record lots of results clearly. Make sure you record when you did your experiments, and anything you might have changed along the way to improve them. No detail is too small when it comes to scientific research.

There are tips for making a great report with each investigation and at the end of this book. Use them as guides and don't be afraid to be creative. Make it *your* investigation!

Pink vinegar and purple water?

In school, you might have mixed bicarbonate of soda with vinegar and seen it bubble. You may even have added food colouring to the mixture and put it inside a homemade volcano (see picture above). Vinegar is an **acid,** and bicarbonate of soda is a **base.** When they react together, they make bubbles. Learn which everyday substances are acids and which are bases through this experiment.

Do your research

This project looks at acids and bases. The **pH** scale measures how acidic or basic a substance is. The scale goes from 0 to 14. Strong acids have a pH of 2 or below. Bases, which are the opposite of acids, are at the other end of the pH scale. They can have a pH as high as 14. Pure water, which is neither an acid nor a base, has a pH of 7, which means that it is neutral. (Rainwater, however, is usually a little acidic as a result of natural minerals or pollution.) Do some research on acids and bases and on the pH of various liquids. After you've done some research, you'll be ready to try this project. Of course, you might want to come up with your own project.

Here are some books and websites you could start with in your research:

» *Material Matters: Acids and Bases*, Carol Baldwin (Raintree, 2004)
» *Changing Materials*, Robert Snedden (Heinemann Library, 2007)
» Acids and bases are everywhere:
   http://www.chem4kids.com/files/react_acidbase.html
» Red cabbage indicator: http://www.lmpc.edu.au/Resources/Science/
   indicator&solutions/solutions.htm

Background information

Possible question

Which substances are acids, and which substances are bases?

Possible hypothesis

Lemon and orange juice are acids, and soaps are bases.

Level of difficulty

Advanced

Approximate cost of materials

£9.00

Materials needed

» One head of red cabbage (find this in the produce section of the super-market. Make sure it is red cabbage; white cabbage does not work.)

» One 2-litre (3.5-pint) saucepan

Materials needed (cont.)

» Water
» Hob top or gas ring
» Oven gloves
» Fork or metal tongs
» Nine clear glasses
» Clear vinegar
» Masking tape and a pen
» Washing-up liquid
» Distilled water (found in the bottled water aisle of the supermarket)
» Various kitchen liquids, such as juices and fizzy drinks (colourless or light-coloured liquids work best)
» Various cleansers, such as shampoo, bicarbonate of soda, and liquid soap. **Do not use household cleaners that contain bleach or ammonia, because these can cause burns.**
» Adult supervisor

Outline of methods

1. Tear off about 10 cabbage leaves and put them in the saucepan. Add enough water to cover the leaves.

2. **Caution: Ask an adult to help when using the hob top and hot water.** Put your saucepan on a hob top or gas ring. Turn it to a high setting.

ADULT SUPERVISION REQUIRED

Continued

3. Heat the water until it boils – the water should be bubbling. Turn the heat down and let the water simmer for 15 minutes. The water will turn purple.

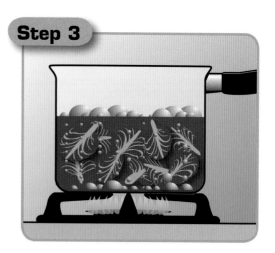

Step 3

4. After 15 minutes, turn off the heat. Put on oven gloves and remove the pan from the ring. Allow the water to cool in the pan for about 30 minutes.

5. Remove the leaves with a fork or metal tongs and throw the leaves away.

6. Carefully pour the cabbage juice into each of the nine glasses, filling them about one-quarter full. You will use the juice as your pH indicator.

7. Fill one of the glasses with vinegar to the halfway point. Observe the colour of the contents. Use masking tape and a pen to label the glass Vinegar.

8. Repeat step 7 with washing-up liquid and with distilled water. Make sure you label each glass. You should now have three different colours. Vinegar is an acid with a pH of about 3; washing-up liquid is a base with a pH of about 8; and water is considered neutral, with a pH of about 7. These three liquids can be used for comparisons with your other substances. (Stronger acids and bases are dangerous to handle, so do not use them in the experiment.)

Step 8

Vinegar

Washing-up liquid

Distilled water

9. Fill the other glasses containing the cabbage juice with the other substances you want to test. Make sure you label the glasses with the names of the substances.

10. Place the glasses in order of colour, starting with the pink liquids and working toward the green liquids. This will also place the liquids in order from acids to bases.

Analysis of results

» Which substance was closest in colour to the vinegar?
» Which substance was closest in colour to the washing-up liquid?
» Which substance was closest in colour to the distilled water?
» Which substances would be considered acids?
» Which substances would be considered bases?

More activities to extend your investigation

» Use your cabbage juice pH indicator to test different bottled waters and tap water to see the difference in pH.
» Repeat the experiment using different fizzy drinks, such as lemon and lime versus cream soda, or diet drinks versus non-diet drinks.
» Repeat the experiment comparing different brands or types of shampoos.

Project extras

» Take a photograph or draw an illustration of the cups in colour order. Write the pH values next to the appropriate colours.
» Create a poster of your project. You could draw a border by repeating the sequence of colours that you obtained in your project.

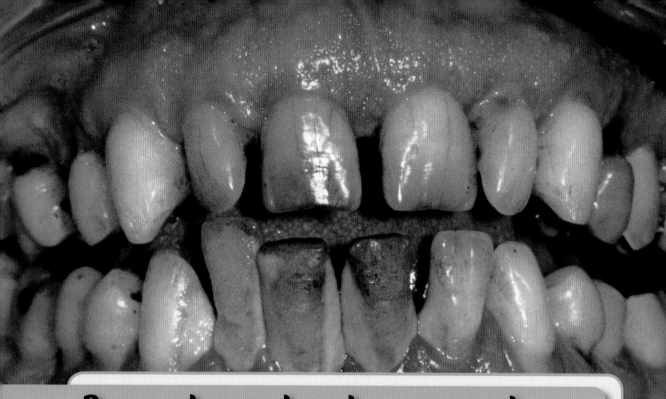

Remember to brush your teeth

What's so bad about not brushing your teeth? Over time, foods and drinks that contain acids can eat away at the surface of your teeth. This is called **demineralisation**. Brushing your teeth helps to prevent demineralisation. Teeth contain **calcium** – a substance that helps keep them strong. The shell of an egg is also made of calcium. In this experiment you will test the effect of different liquids on eggshells.

Do your research

Learn about the **element** calcium. Where is it found? Why is it important? We know the surfaces of teeth contain calcium, so you might want to find out about the structure of teeth. You will be comparing different liquids, so try to find out what is in them. For instance, fizzy drinks contain **phosphoric acid.** What else do drinks contain? After you've done some research, you'll be ready to try this project. Or, you may want to come up with your own unique project.

Background information

Possible question

Which liquids cause eggshells to soften: vinegar, cola, coffee, water?

Possible hypothesis

Vinegar will cause the eggshells to soften because it is an acid.

Level of difficulty

Easy

Approximate cost of materials

£4.00

Materials needed

» Five jars with lids (each large enough to hold an egg)
» Clear vinegar
» Cola soft drink (dark-coloured fizzy drink, not diet)
» Black coffee (made and cooled)
» Water
» Masking tape
» Marker pen
» Five uncooked white-shelled eggs
» Rubber gloves

Here are some books and websites you could start with in your research:

» *Calcium and the Alkaline Earth Metals*, Nigel Saunders (Heinemann Library, 2003)
» *Calcium*, Salvatore Tocci (Children's Press, 2004)
» Calcium: http://www.vegsoc.org/info/calcium.html
» Calcium: http://www.chemsoc.org/viselements/pages/calcium.html
» Teeth: http://www.healthyteeth.org

Outline of methods

1. Fill each jar two-thirds full with one of the following liquids: vinegar, cola, coffee, and water. Leave one jar empty. The empty jar is your control.

Continued

2. Put a strip of masking tape on each jar and write the name of the liquid it contains.

3. Place one egg in each jar. Make sure you do this gently so that you don't break the egg. Put on the lid to seal the jar shut.

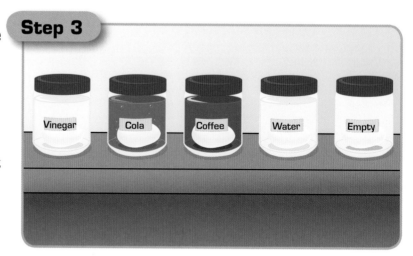

Step 3

Vinegar Cola Coffee Water Empty

4. Leave the jars to sit for approximately 24 hours at room temperature.

5. Create a results table similar to the one below.

	Vinegar	Cola	Coffee	Water	Empty (Control)
What does the eggshell look like?					
What does the eggshell feel like?					
What does the liquid look like?					

6. Put on your rubber gloves. Carefully examine the shell of each egg. If there is no difference in the eggshells, leave them for another day or two.

7. When one or more of the eggshells appear to have changed, fill in your chart with descriptions of how the shell looks and feels, as well as what the liquid looks like.

Analysis of results

» Which liquid(s) changed the look of the eggshell?

» Which liquid(s) changed the way the eggshell felt?

» What happened to the liquid in each jar?

More activities to extend your investigation

» To test how toothpaste protects the teeth, use an old toothbrush to rub some on one egg. Use a clean egg as a control. Put each egg in a jar of vinegar and compare the eggshells after a day or two.

» Try using other drinks or sugar water. You can vary the amount of sugar in the water and determine whether the concentration of sugar affects the eggshell.

» Try using diet drinks and non-diet drinks to see how this affects your results.

Project extras

» Take a photograph or draw an illustration of how the eggs looked at the end of the project.

» Include the table you created.

The best biscuit recipe

When you bake biscuit dough, the ingredients undergo chemical reactions in the oven to create delicious biscuits. But why are chocolate chip biscuits so appealing? Is it the chocolate chips? The sugar? In this experiment, you will find out by altering the ingredients.

Do your research

Chocolate chip biscuits have an interesting history. You might want to research when they were first made. Do some research about each of the ingredients in biscuits and about the chemical changes that happen as the biscuits bake. Your research may give you an idea of which ingredient you want to change. After you've done your research, you'll be ready to start this project. Or, your research may lead you to come up with your own unique project.

Here are some books and websites you could start with in your research:

» *Material Matters: Chemical Reactions*, Carol Baldwin (Raintree, 2004)

» *Science@School: Changing Materials*, Brian Knapp (Atlantic Europe Publishing, 2003)

» Chocolate-chip cookies: http://en.wikipedia.org/wiki/Chocolate_chip_cookies

Background information

Possible question

Why do people use bicarbonate of soda in chocolate chip biscuits?

Possible hypothesis

Bicarbonate of soda helps biscuits rise when they are baked in an oven.

Level of difficulty

Advanced

Approximate cost of materials

£12.00

Materials needed

» Oven » Small mixing bowl
» Electric mixer or a wooden spoon

Materials needed (cont.)

» 180 grams (6 ounces) butter or margarine
» Kitchen scales and a measuring spoon
» 90 grams (3 ounces) white sugar
» 90 grams (3 ounces) brown sugar
» Vanilla extract
» Two eggs, beaten together
» 210 grams (7.5 ounces) flour
» Bicarbonate of soda (not baking powder)
» Salt
» 180 grams (6 ounces) choc chips
» Tablespoon   » Baking tray
» Oven gloves   » Cooling rack
» Spatula   » Adult supervisor

Outline of methods

1. Choose one ingredient that you would like to test so that you can find out how it changes the biscuits. Create a table like this one to record the data.

	Batch 1 Control recipe	Batch 2 Less bicarbonate of soda	Batch 3 More bicarbonate of soda
Physical characteristics			
Texture			
Taste			

Continued

2. Follow the biscuit recipe to create Batch 1. This is your control.

a. Caution: Ask an adult to help you use the oven.

Preheat the oven to 190 °C (375 °F). Place 60 grams (2 ounces) butter, 30 grams (1 ounce) white sugar, 30 grams (1 ounce) brown sugar, and 1.2 millilitres (¼ teaspoon) vanilla extract in a bowl and mix well.

b. Add ½ beaten egg (approximately 1½ tablespoons) and mix again.

c. Mix in 70 grams (2.5 ounces) flour, 1.2 millilitres (¼ teaspoon) bicarbonate of soda, and 1.2 millilitres (¼ teaspoon) salt. Last, stir in 60 grams (2 ounces) choc chips. Do not eat the uncooked dough, because it contains raw eggs.

d. Use a tablespoon to scoop spoonfuls of the dough onto an ungreased baking tray. Leave about 2.5 centimetres (1 inch) between the biscuits.

e. Caution: Ask an adult to help you use the oven.

Place the baking tray in the oven on the middle rack and bake for nine to eleven minutes.

f. When the biscuits are golden, put on oven gloves and take the biscuits out of the oven. Use a spatula to carefully remove them from the tray and put them on a cooling rack.

Step 2d

3. Allow the biscuits to cool for 15 minutes.

4. Choose someone to test your biscuits. Make sure you ask whether the person has any food allergies. Your tester must have no allergies to any of the ingredients.

5. Get your tester to try the biscuits but do not tell him or her whether you changed an ingredient. This is called a **blind test.**

6. Repeat steps 2 to 5 using the same recipe, but with less of your chosen ingredient. This is Batch 2.

7. Repeat steps 2 to 5 using the same recipe, but with more of your chosen ingredient. This is Batch 3.

Analysis of results

» Examine the biscuits from each batch. Are they different colours? Measure the thickness – are some flatter or puffier? Write your observations in the Physical Characteristics row of the table.

» Look at the texture of the biscuits. Break one of each kind open. Are they crisp or soft? Write your observations in the Texture row of the table.

» Get your testers to take a bite of each kind of biscuit. What is the difference in the taste? Is one sweeter than the rest? Too salty? Too bland? Write their observations in the Taste row of the table.

More activities to extend your investigation

» Test whether the oven temperature affects biscuit flavour, texture, and baking time.

» Experiment with melted versus softened butter to see how that variable makes a difference.

Project extras

» Take a picture of each batch of biscuits.

» Include your data table in your report.

» Include a summary of the history of chocolate chip biscuits.

Mystery mixture

You've probably learned about the three main states of matter – liquid, solid, and gas. Each state has unique properties, or characteristics. In this experiment, you will create a squishy, stretchy substance and decide which state of matter it resembles the most.

Do your research

The squishy substance you will make is a **polymer.** Polymers are made up of long chains of tiny molecules. Some polymers are hard and stiff; others are soft and flexible. Plastics and rubbers are polymers. The mixture you are making is also a colloid. Find out more about colloids, the properties of different polymers, and the properties of solids and liquids. After you've done your research, you'll be ready to start this project. Or, your research may lead you to try something else.

In this experiment you will use a laundry chemical called borax. If your skin is sensitive to cleansers, you may want to choose a different project. Wash your hands after you finish conducting the experiment. Make sure you store the borax away from small children, pets, and food. Wash down surfaces after you have used borax. Never put substances that contain borax in your mouth.

Background information

Possible question

Is the polymer a solid or a liquid?

Possible hypothesis

The polymer is a liquid.

Level of difficulty

Intermediate

Approximate cost of materials

£4.00

Materials needed

» A glass of water » A rubber ball
» A jar or container with a lid
» Safety goggles
» 235 millilitres (8 fl.oz) warm water
» 235 millilitres (8 fl.oz.) white glue
» An old, medium-size bowl
» A wooden or plastic spoon
» 80 millilitres (2.5 fl.oz) warm water
» A measuring spoon
» 5 millilitres (1 teaspoon) borax
   (found online or in chemists)
» A measuring jug
» Food colouring (optional)
» Adult supervisor

Here are some books and websites you could start with in your research:

» *Science@School: Changing from Solids to Liquids to Gases*, Brian Knapp (Atlantic Europe Publishing, 2002)
» *Chemicals in Action: States of Matter*, Chris Oxlade (Heinemann Library, 2007)
» States of matter: http://www.harcourtschool.com/activity/states_of_matter
» Three states of matter: http://www.schoolscience.co.uk/content/3/chemistry/materials/match1pg2.html
» Polymers: http://pslc.ws/macrog/kidsmac/basics.htm

Outline of methods

1. Create a table to record the data, similar to the one on the next page.

Continued

	Water (Liquid)	Ball (Solid)	Mystery mixture
Does it flow?			
Does it take the shape of a container?			
Does it hold a shape when not in a container?			
Does it bounce?			

2. First, test the water by following these steps:
    a. Observe the water in the glass. Does it take the shape of the glass?
    b. Pour the water into a sink. Does it flow?
    c. Pour a small amount of the water onto a hard, flat surface, such as a kitchen work surface. Does the water hold its shape? When it lands on the surface, does it bounce?
    d. Fill in the Water column of the table.

3. Next, test the rubber ball by following these steps:
    a. Tip the rubber ball from your hands into the sink. Does it flow?
    b. Put the ball into the container. Does it take the shape of the container?
    c. Drop the ball onto the hard, flat surface.
    Does the ball keep its shape? Does it bounce?
    d. Fill in the Ball column of the table.

ADULT SUPERVISION REQUIRED

4. **Caution: Ask an adult to help you when using borax. Carefully read the safety advice on page 20.**
    Follow these instructions to make the polymer:
    a. Put on your safety goggles. Put 235 millilitres (8 fluid ounces) warm water and 235 millilitres (8 fluid ounces) white glue in a bowl. Mix well using a spoon.
    b. Put 80 millilitres (2.5 fluid ounces) warm water and 5 millilitres (1 teaspoon) borax in a jar and seal with the lid. Shake the mixture to combine the ingredients. Add a few of drops of food colouring (optional) and shake again.
    c. Pour the borax solution into the bowl with the glue and water.
    d. Mix the ingredients together with your hands.

5. To test the polymer:
a. Pour the polymer into the sink. Does it flow?
b. Put the polymer into the container. Does it take the shape of the container?
c. Drop the polymer onto the hard, flat surface. Does it keep its shape? Does it bounce?
d. Fill in the Mystery Mixture column. When you are finished, throw away the polymer in the bin. Clean all the surfaces that touched the borax; then wash your hands.

Step 5

Analysis of results

» Did the polymer have more properties of a solid or a liquid?
» What are some unique properties of the polymer?

More activities to extend your investigation

» Change the amount of glue or water and see how this affects the consistency of the polymer.
» Use cold water instead of warm water. Does this alter the polymer?

Project extras

» Take photographs of your polymer and include these in your report.
» Include information on other polymers and how they compare to the polymer you created.

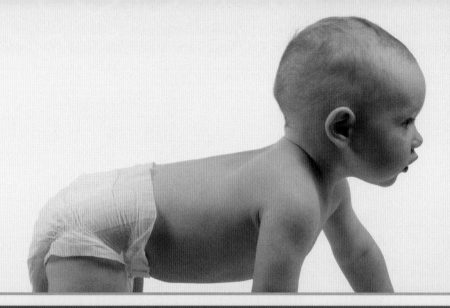

Time to change the nappy

Have you ever seen a baby go swimming while wearing a normal, disposable nappy instead of a swim nappy? The nappy ends up looking like a big, heavy balloon. There is a chemical in disposable nappies called sodium polyacrylate, which absorbs water. We all know that water isn't what normally goes into nappies. Urine is not pure water – it contains salts. You will test different salt concentrations to see how well the nappy absorbs each sample.

Do your research

In this experiment, you will test how well sodium polyacrylate absorbs tap water and salt water. Find out some more about sodium polyacrylate and do some research on sodium chloride, the salt you will use. After you've done your research, you'll be ready to start this project. Or, your research may lead you to try something else.

You could start your research using this book and these websites:

» *Sodium*, Anne O'Daly (Benchmark Books, 2002)
» Sodium polyacrylate: http://home.howstuffworks.com/question207.htm
» Sodium: http://www.chemsoc.org/VISELEMENTS/pages/sodium.html

Background information

Possible question

Do nappies absorb salt solutions as well as they do water?

Possible hypothesis

Nappies do not absorb salt solutions as well as they do water.

Level of difficulty

Intermediate

Approximate cost of materials

£5.00

Materials needed

» Water
» A measuring jug
» Three containers – 1 litre or 2 pints, or bigger
» Masking tape and a pen
» Table salt (table salt contains sodium chloride)
» Spoon
» A package of normal, disposable nappies
» Stopwatch

Outline of methods

1. Measure 1 litre of water and put it in the first container. Add 100 grams of salt and mix thoroughly. (Or add 4 ounces of salt to 2 pints of water.) Label this 10% Salt Solution.

2. Repeat step 1, but this time put 200 grams salt in 1 litre of water. (Or add 8 ounces of salt to 2 pints of water.) Label this 20% Salt Solution.

3. Fill the third container with tap water. Label it Tap Water.

4. Lay out three of the nappies and fold back the leg openings.

Step 4

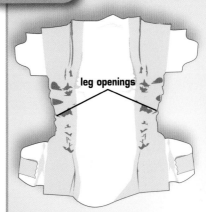

leg openings

Fold out the leg openings so that the nappy lies flat.

Continued

5. Use masking tape and the marker to label the three nappies Tap Water. Put the labels on the edge of the nappies.

6. Create a table to record the data, similar to the one below. (You will do three trials with each salt solution.)

	Trial one	Trial two	Trial three	Average
Tap water				
10% salt solution				
20% salt solution				

7. Measure 120 millilitres (4 fluid ounces) of tap water. Pour it in the centre of one of the nappies. Start the stopwatch and time 10 seconds. If there is no liquid on the surface of the nappy, put a tally mark on the data table next to Tap Water in the column for Trial One.

8. Add another 120 millilitres (4 fluid ounces) of tap water and repeat the procedure. If the nappy doesn't leak, add another tally mark next to the first.

9. Repeat this procedure until water is no longer absorbed into the nappy after 10 seconds. When this happens, do not record any more tally marks. (Some water may be caught in the leg ruffle – do not count that as water that is not absorbed.)

10. Repeat steps 7 to 9 with two other nappies labelled Tap Water. Observe and record the amount of liquid the nappy absorbed, making tally marks in the Trial Two and Trial Three columns of the Tap Water row.

11. Calculate how many millilitres (or fluid ounces) the nappy absorbed in each trial. Remember that one tally mark = 120 millilitres (4 fluid ounces).

12. Take an average by adding the three amounts together, and dividing that number by three (since there were three numbers added together.) This is the average amount of water the nappies absorbed. In any experiment, it's best to repeat the test at least three times and take an average. This compensates for human errors and any differences in the materials used.

13. Open out three new nappies and label them 10% Salt Solution. Repeat steps 7 to 12 using the 10% salt solution instead of the tap water. Write your results in the appropriate part of the table.

14. Last, open three new nappies and label them 20% Salt Solution. Repeat steps 7 to 12 using the 20% salt solution. Write your results in the appropriate part of the table.

Analysis of results

» Which salt solution did the nappies absorb the best?
» Which salt solution did the nappies absorb the worst?

More activities to extend your investigation

» Compare different nappy brands to see which absorbs best (use only one type of liquid, such as tap water OR a salt solution).
» Compare the amount of liquid absorbed by a cloth nappy and a disposable nappy.

Project extras

» Take a photograph of the total amount of water each nappy held. Label the photos and include them in your report.
» Draw a bar graph of the average amount of liquid each nappy held.
» Include a copy of your data table in your report.

It's freezing in here!

Temperatures are different around the world. At the North and South Poles, temperatures can be very cold. Even though temperatures can go below 0 °C (32 °F), the sea doesn't always freeze solid. One reason for this is that there is salt in the seawater. Learn about the **freezing points** of different liquids through this experiment.

Do your research

Elements found in nature are organised into a table, called the **periodic table.** Research the freezing points of common **elements,** such as iron and carbon. Also, read about the properties of water – what happens to the water molecules when water freezes? After you've done your research, you'll be ready to start this project. Or, you may decide to come up with your own unique project.

Here are some books and websites you could start with in your research:

» *Chemicals In Action: States of Matter*, Chris Oxlade (Heinemann Library, 2007)
» *The Periodic Table*, Salvatore Tocci (Children's Press, 2004)
» Matter: http://www.chem4kids.com/files/matter_intro.html
» States of matter: http://www.harcourtschool.com/activity/states_of_matter
» Changing states: http://www.bbc.co.uk/schools/scienceclips/ages/9_10/changing_state.shtml
» Freezing point: http://www.schoolscience.co.uk/content/3/chemistry/materials/match1pg2.html

Background information

Possible question

Which liquids have lower freezing points than that of water?

Possible hypothesis

Vegetable oil has a lower freezing point than water does.

Level of difficulty

Easy

Approximate cost of materials

£11.00

Materials needed

» Four clear plastic cups
» A measuring jug and scales
» Salt » Water
» Spoon » Masking tape
» Marker » Orange juice
» Vegetable oil
» Four alcohol thermometers (Make sure the thermometers can reach below 0°C (32°F). Do not use mercury thermometers – the liquid inside is not safe.)
» A freezer

Outline of methods

1. Create a salt water solution by mixing 60 grams (2 ounces) salt with 180 millilitres (6 fluid ounces) warm water in a plastic cup. Stir the solution until the salt dissolves and then let it sit. Label the cup Salt Water.

2. Measure 240 millilitres (8 fluid ounces) of tap water and pour it into a second plastic cup. Label the cup Water. Do the same for both the orange juice and the vegetable oil.

3. Put a thermometer in each cup and let them sit for about one hour. This ensures that the liquids are at the same temperature before they are put into the freezer.

4. Draw a table similar to the one on the next page. Record the starting temperature of each sample. Observe the samples and fill in the state of each (liquid, partially liquid, or solid).

Continued

	Salt water		Water		Orange juice		Vegetable oil	
	Temp	State	Temp	State	Temp	State	Temp	State
Beginning of the experiment								
20 minutes								
40 minutes								
1 hour								
1 hour, 20 minutes								
1 hour, 40 minutes								
2 hours								

5. Place all four cups in the freezer with the labels and thermometers facing out.

6. Check the substances every 20 minutes and fill in your table.

7. You may also want to let the cups freeze overnight and observe them the next day.

Step 5

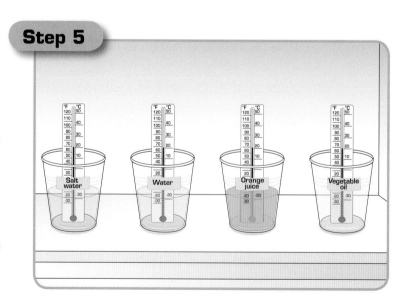

Analysis of results

» What was the freezing temperature of each of the liquids?

» Were there any other changes to any of the liquids?

» Which liquid froze solid first?

» Which liquid took the longest to freeze?

» Were there any liquids that didn't freeze?

More activities to extend your investigation

» Compare the temperatures at which different concentrations of salt water freeze.

» Compare the melting temperatures of different solids, such as flavoured ice pops and ice.

Project extras

» Take photographs or draw illustrations of the cups of liquid before and after freezing.

» Create a list of liquids that freeze at a temperature lower than that of water. List common uses for those liquids.

Salty seawater has a lower freezing point than that of freshwater.

Why is the Statue of Liberty green?

Have you ever noticed that the Statue of Liberty looks blue-green? Just as certain metals rust and turn brown, others turn a whitish colour, or even green. Compare what happens to different metals when put in a salt-and-vinegar solution.

Do your research

Pennies are coated with copper. When combined with other chemicals, such as an acid and salt, the copper **oxidizes.** The process of oxidation is similar to rusting. A blue-green substance, called a **precipitate,** forms on the copper's surface.

In this project, you will use vinegar, which is an acid, and salt, which contains sodium chloride. Before you begin, you may want to read more about vinegar and sodium chloride. You may also want to read more about the properties of copper and other metals. Once you've done some research, you are ready to begin this project. Or, you may come up with your own project after you've read and learned more about the topic.

Background information

Possible question

What will happen to metal washers when exposed to a salt-and-vinegar solution?

Possible hypothesis

Copper washers will oxidize because the copper will react with a salt-and-vinegar solution.

Level of difficulty

Intermediate

Approximate cost of materials

£2.00

Materials needed

» Plastic gloves
» Measuring jug
» Vinegar
» Salt
» Tablespoon
» Empty plastic egg carton or three other small containers
» Marker pen
» Six of each kind of a variety of metal washers, such as steel, bronze, and copper (You can buy washers at a hardware shop.)
» Kitchen towel

Here are some books and websites you could start with in your research:

» *Sodium*, Anne O'Daly (Benchmark Books, 2002)
» *Chemicals in Action: Elements and Compounds*, Chris Oxlade (Heinemann Library, 2007)
» *Copper*, Salvatore Tocci (Children's Press, 2005)
» The reactivity series: http://www.bbc.co.uk/schools/ks3bitesize/science/chemistry/m_m_chem_props_1.shtml
» Copper: http://www.chemsoc.org/viselements/pages/copper.html

Outline of methods

1. **Put on plastic gloves.** It is important to wear gloves while setting up this experiment and when touching the solution.

2. Measure 60 millilitres (2 fluid ounces) vinegar and add 15 millilitres (1 tablespoon) salt. Stir the solution until the salt dissolves.

  Continued

3. Label the outside of three sections of the egg carton with the type of metal washer.

4. Place one of each kind of metal washer in the appropriate section of the egg carton.

5. Pour the solution over each washer. Leave the washers to stand in the solution for 10 minutes.

Step 5

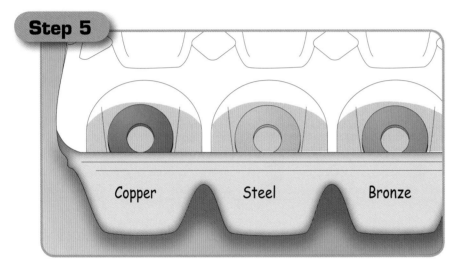

Copper   Steel   Bronze

6. Take out the washers and lay them on the flat surface of the egg carton or on a piece of kitchen towel. Write the name of each metal on the egg carton or kitchen towel, close to each washer.

7. Leave the washers to dry for one hour.

8. Compare each washer with the one that wasn't put in the solution. The washers that were not put in solution are your controls.

Step 6

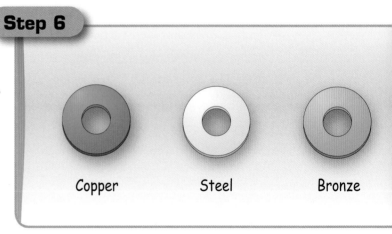

Copper   Steel   Bronze

9. Repeat the experiment twice, using new washers and fresh salt-and-vinegar solution each time. By repeating the experiment, you increase the accuracy of your results.

Analysis of results

» What happened to each washer that was in the solution?
» Which washers were covered with a precipitate?
» What did each solution look like after the washer had been in it?

More activities to extend your investigation

» Carry out the experiment using other metal objects, such as different metal coins. You will need to find out exactly what each coin is made from – the composition will vary depending on when each coin was made.
» Use only one type of washer and compare what happens in different acids, such as orange juice and lemon juice.
» Use just one type of metal and observe what happens in different liquids, such as salt water and tap water.

Project extras:

» Draw a picture of each object at the end of the experiment.
» Include a table of your data.

What a gas!

Nobody enjoys an upset stomach. **Antacid** tablets are used to lower the amount of acid in the stomach to make you feel better. They contain calcium carbonate, which is a base. When a base is combined with an acid, a gas is produced. In this experiment, you will combine antacid tablets with water in a sealed container. This will produce **carbon dioxide** gas. You will experiment to see whether the amount of antacid makes a difference in the amount of gas that forms.

Do your research

In this experiment, you will collect carbon dioxide gas in a balloon placed on top of a plastic bottle. When you produce gas in a sealed container, the pressure builds up. The extra pressure causes the balloon to inflate. This experiment can be messy, so move nearby objects out of the way. Make sure you wear safety goggles to protect your eyes. Never take antacid tablets unless they are prescribed for you by a qualified doctor or chemist, and always read the packet label to find the correct dose.

Do some research about carbon dioxide gas. You may also want to find out how antacids work. Once you've done some research, you can get into this project or you can create your own unique project.

Background information

Possible question

Does the amount of **effervescent** (fizzy) antacid tablet affect the amount of carbon dioxide gas produced?

Possible hypothesis

The more antacid tablet used, the more carbon dioxide gas is produced.

Level of difficulty

Easy

Approximate cost of materials

£7.00

Materials needed

» A pack of 25-centimetre (10-inch) balloons
» Three empty plastic water bottles (about 500 millilitres or 1 pint in size)
» An assistant
» Two pairs of safety goggles (Most hardware shops sell them, or you may be able to borrow them from your science teacher.)
» Two sets of plastic gloves
» Effervescent antacid tablets
» A measuring jug
» Water
» A stopwatch
» A tape measure

Here are some books and websites you could start with in your research:

» *Science@School: Changing Materials*, Brian Knapp (Atlantic Europe Publishing, 2003)
» *Science@School: Gases Around Us*, Brian Knapp (Atlantic Europe Publishing, 2002)
» How do antacids work?: http://gerd.emedtv.com/antacids/antacids.html
» Stomach acid and carbon dioxide: http://www.planet-science.com/outthere/index.html?page=/outthere/diner/play/02.html

Continued

Outline of methods

1. Stretch out the openings of the balloons. You might also want to practise fitting a balloon over the opening of a water bottle. It needs to be placed over the grooves on the top of the water bottle so that no gas escapes.

2. You and your assistant need to put on your safety goggles and plastic gloves.

3. Put one half of an antacid tablet in a water bottle.

4. Measure 60 millilitres (2 fluid ounces) of water and add this to the water bottle. Quickly cover the top of the bottle with a balloon. The gas produced should inflate the balloon. If necessary, help the balloon stand up.

Step 4

5. After 30 seconds, ask your assistant to use a tape measure to measure the widest part of the balloon as you hold it in place.

Step 5

6. Carefully remove the balloon from the bottle by holding on to the balloon's neck and slowly pulling it off of the bottle. Discard the balloon. Record your results.

7. Do the experiment two more times using half a tablet. Then, average your three measurements by adding them together and dividing by three. Record the average measurement.

8. Repeat steps 3 to 7 with one whole tablet (you may need to break it in half to fit it in the bottle). Continue to use the same amount of water – vary only the amount of antacid tablet.

9. Last, repeat steps 3 to 7 with two whole tablets. When you finish the experiment, discard the empty water bottles.

Analysis of results

» Which amount of antacid produced the most carbon dioxide?
» Which amount of antacid produced the least carbon dioxide?
» What did the antacid look like after the reaction?

More activities to extend your investigation

» Try the experiment again, but this time substitute lemon juice for water.
» Change the amount of water instead of changing the amount of antacid.
» Test different brands of effervescent tablet (using only one tablet) and compare the size of the balloon for each. Keep the amount of water the same.
» Change the temperature of the water to see whether that affects the amount of carbon dioxide produced.

Project extras

» Create a bar graph of your results.
» Create a table to show your results.

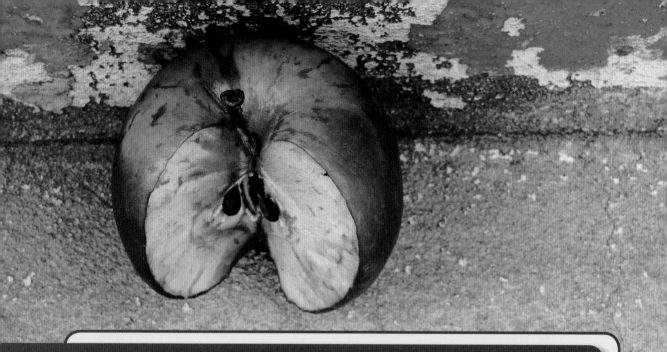

A sour saver

Don't you hate it when you cut up an apple, sit down to eat it, and find it has already turned brown? Cut fruits, such as apples, quickly oxidize and turn brown when exposed to air. Is there a way to prevent them from browning? In this project, you will experiment with lemon juice and water to see whether covering the surface of an apple with those liquids prevents the apple from browning.

Do your research

Find out more about why fruit browns. Cooks often use foods containing acids, such as lemon juice, to prevent fruit from browning. Learn more about this topic by researching oxidation and food preservation. Once you've done some research, you can get into this project or you can create your own unique project.

You could start your research using this book and these websites:

» *Material Matters: Chemical Reactions*, Carol Baldwin (Raintree, 2005)
» Why does fruit brown?: http://www.geocities.com/perfectapple/brown.html
» Oxidation of foods: http://www.bbc.co.uk/schools/gcsebitesize/design/ foodtech/acidoxitemprev3.shtml

Background information

Possible question

Will coating a cut apple with water or lemon juice slow the browning process?

Possible hypothesis

Coating a cut apple with lemon juice will slow the browning process.

Level of difficulty

Easy

Approximate cost of materials

£2.50

Materials needed

» Two bowls
» Lemon juice (you can either squeeze the juice from a lemon or buy lemon juice)
» Water
» Waxed or greaseproof paper
» Masking tape
» Marker pen
» Three apples
» A butter knife
» A chopping board
» Adult supervisor

Outline of methods

1. Pour enough lemon juice in a bowl to cover the bottom of the bowl. Fill a second bowl with the same amount of water.

2. Lay out a sheet of waxed or greaseproof paper. With the tape and marker, create three labels – Lemon Juice, Water, and Control. (Your control piece will be a slice of apple with nothing on it.)

3. **Caution: Either get permission to use a knife or ask an adult to cut the apple for you.** Cut an apple into equal-sized pieces.

ADULT SUPERVISION REQUIRED

4. Dip one piece of apple in the lemon juice, coating the sides of the apple without the peel. Place it on the paper near the Lemon Juice label.

 Continued

5. Dip a second piece of apple in the water, coating the sides of the apple without peel. Place it on the paper near the Water label.

6. Place a third piece of apple on the paper near the Control label.

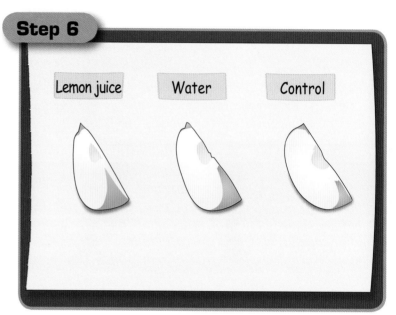

Step 6

Lemon juice   Water   Control

7. Check the apple pieces every 20 minutes for browning. Create a chart like the one below and note the appearance of the apple pieces (not at all brown, slightly discoloured, brown, very brown).

	Lemon juice	Water	Control
20 minutes			
40 minutes			
1 hour			
1 hour, 20 minutes			
1 hour, 40 minutes			
2 hours			

8. It is important that you do not eat the apples after performing the experiment. Make sure you throw all of the apple pieces away immediately after the experiment.

9. Repeat the experiment twice, using new apples and fresh liquids each time. Repeating the experiment increases the accuracy of your results.

Analysis of results

» Which apple piece started to turn brown first?

» Which apple piece took the longest to brown?

» Which apple piece ended up the most brown?

» Which apple piece ended up the least brown?

» Did any of the apple pieces not brown at all?

More activities to extend your investigation

» Compare different types of apple to see whether one variety browns faster than another.

» Test whether freezing or refrigerating apple pieces prevents them from browning.

» Experiment with different liquids including salt water, vinegar and cola to see whether they prevent browning.

» Find out which other fruits and vegetables brown and compare how quickly the process happens.

Project extras

» Include photos of the apple pieces at various times during the experiment.

» Include your data table in your report.

Writing your report

In many ways, writing the report of your investigation is the hardest part. You've researched the science involved, and you've had fun gathering all your evidence together. Now you have to explain what it's all about.

You are the expert

Very few other people, if any, will have done your investigation. So you are the expert here. You need to explain your ideas clearly. Scientists get their most important investigations published in a scientific magazine or journal. They may also stand up at meetings and tell other scientists what they have found. Or they may display a large poster to explain their investigation. You might consider giving a talk or making a poster about your investigation, too. But however scientists present their investigations, they always write it down first – and you must too. Here are some tips about what you should include in your report.

Some hints for collecting your results

» **Making a table:** Tables are great for recording lots of results. Use a pencil and ruler to draw your table lines, or make a table using a word processing program. Put the units (m, s, kg, N and so on) in the headings only. Don't write them into the main body of your table. Try to make your table fit one side of paper. If you need two sheets of paper, make sure you write the column headings on the second sheet as well.

» **Recording your results:** It is often easy to forget to write down your results as they come in. Or you might just scribble them onto the back of your hand, and then wash your hands! A wise scientist will always make a neat, blank table in their lab book before starting. They will write down their results as they go along and not later on.

» **Odd stuff:** If something goes wrong, make a note of it. This will remind you which results might not be reliable.

» **Precision:** Always record your readings to the precision of your measuring equipment. For example, if you have scales that show 24.6 g, don't write 24 or 25 in your table. Instead, write 24.6 because that's the precise measurement.

Laying out your report

You could use the following headings to organise your report in a clear manner:

» **A title**
This gives an idea of what your investigation is about.

» **Aims**
Write a brief outline of what you were trying to do. It should include the question you were trying to answer.

» **Hypothesis**
This is your scientific prediction of what will happen in your investigation. Include notes from your research to explain why you think your prediction will work out. It might help to write it out as: "I think ... will happen because ..."

» **Materials**
List the equipment you used to carry out your experiments. Also say what any measuring equipment was for. For example, "scales (to weigh the objects)".

» **Methods**
Explain what you actually did in your investigation.

» **Results**
Record your results, readings, and observations clearly.

» **Conclusions**
Explain how closely your results fitted your hypothesis. You can find out more about this on the next page.

» **Bibliography**
List the books, articles, websites or other resources you used in your research.

And finally ... the conclusions

There are two main bits to your conclusions. These are the "Analysis" and the "Evaluation". In the analysis you explain what your evidence shows, and how it supports or disproves your hypothesis. In the evaluation, you discuss the quality of your results and their reliability, and how successful your methods were.

Your analysis

You need to study your evidence to see if there is a relationship between the variables in your investigation. This can be difficult to spot in a table, so it is a good idea to draw a graph. You should always put the dependent variable on the vertical axis, and the independent variable on the horizontal axis. The type of graph you need to draw depends on the type of variables involved:

» A bar chart if the results are **categoric**, such as hot/cold, male/female.

» A line graph or a scattergram if both variables are **continuous**, such as time, length, or mass.

Remember to label the axes to say what each one shows, and the unit used. For example, "time in s" or "height in cm". Draw a line or curve of best fit if you can.

Explain what your graph shows. Remember that the reader needs help from you to understand your investigation. Even if you have spotted a pattern, don't assume that your reader has. Tell them. For example, "My graph shows that water freezes at a higher temperature than salt water". Circle any points on your graph that seem anomalous (too high or too low).

Your evaluation

Did your investigation go well, or did it go badly? Was your evidence good enough for you to support or disprove your hypothesis? Sometimes it can be difficult for you to answer these questions. But it is really important that you try. Scientists always look back at their investigations. They want to know if they could improve their methods next time. They also want to know if their evidence is reliable and valid. Reliable evidence can be repeated with pretty much the same results. Valid evidence is reliable, and it should answer the question you asked in the first place. As before, remember that you are the person who knows your investigation the best. Don't be afraid to show off valid evidence. And be honest if it's not!

Glossary

accurate close to the true value

acid substance that reacts with certain metals to create salts

antacid substance that makes an acid less acidic

base substance that reacts with acids to form salts

blind test test in which the subject is not aware of the change made to an experiment

calcium metallic element that helps to form strong teeth and bones

carbon dioxide gas in the atmosphere

categoric variable that can be given labels, such as male/female

continuous variable that can have any value, such as weight or length

control something that is left unchanged in order to compare results against it

data factual information

demineralisation loss of minerals

effervescent producing gas as tiny bubbles

element substance that cannot be broken down chemically

evidence data that has been checked to see if it is valid

freezing point temperature at which a liquid turns into a solid

hypothesis scientific idea about how something works, before the idea has been tested

oxidize undergo chemical change as a result of exposure to oxygen

periodic table chart that lists all of the elements

pH a measure of the acidity or alkalinity of a substance

phosphoric acid type of acid found in fertilisers, foods, and detergents

polymer compound made up of repeated, linked units. Natural polymers include rubber and silk; synthetic polymers include plastic and nylon.

precipitate solid that forms from a solution

prediction say in advance what you think will happen, based on scientific study

variable something that can change; is not set or fixed

Index